# Whale Rescue
## *at Cape Cod Bay*

### by Belinda Suarez

Glenview, Illinois • Boston, Massachusetts • Chandler, Arizona
Upper Saddle River, New Jersey

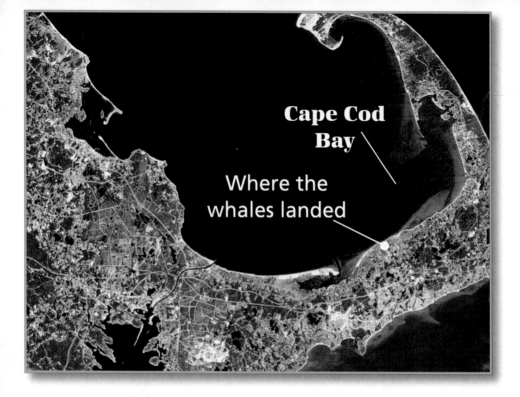

Cape Cod Bay

Where the whales landed

One July morning, in 2002, a group of fifty-six pilot whales became stranded, or stuck, in Cape Cod Bay, Massachusetts. The whales were about a half-mile from shore. It was low tide. The whales were lying on dry ground.

**Did You Know?**  **Ocean Tides**

The tides are the regular rise and fall of ocean water. As the tide comes toward the shore, ocean water covers more of the beach. This is called high tide. Then, for hours, the water level goes down. Water covers less of the beach. This is called low tide.

pilot whale

Pilot whales are dark gray or black. They have rounded heads.

Nobody knows why the whales swam toward the shore. They might have gotten lost while looking for food. They might have been following a school of fish. Maybe they got lost. Scientists could not explain why the whales beached themselves.

---

**school:** a large group of fish swimming together
**beached:** landed on a beach

volunteers

As soon as people heard about the stranded whales, they drove to the beach. A group of almost 2,000 people volunteered to help the whales. Veterinarians and scientists came to help, too.

The volunteers put wet beach towels and sheets over the whales. They had to make sure the whales did not get burned by the sun, or sunburned

---

**veterinarians:** doctors for animals

Whales cannot live on land. When whales are out of the water, their own weight can crush their organs. Whales can't keep their bodies at the right temperature out of the water. They become too hot when they are in the sun. That is why volunteers poured water over the whales and covered them with towels and sheets.

towel

water

Adults and children helped the whales.

---

**organs:** parts inside the body, such as the heart and lungs

While the volunteers waited for the tide to rise, they kept pouring water on the whales to keep them cool. The veterinarians examined the whales to make sure they were alright.

When the tide started to rise, the water reached the whales again. By 2:00 P.M., the whales were beginning to move in the water.

The volunteers wanted to help the whales swim back to the ocean. They beat drums and yelled in order to scare the whales away from the shore and back toward the ocean. They used boats to chase the whales away from the shore. That day, 46 whales returned to the ocean. The volunteers had helped save 46 pilot whales.

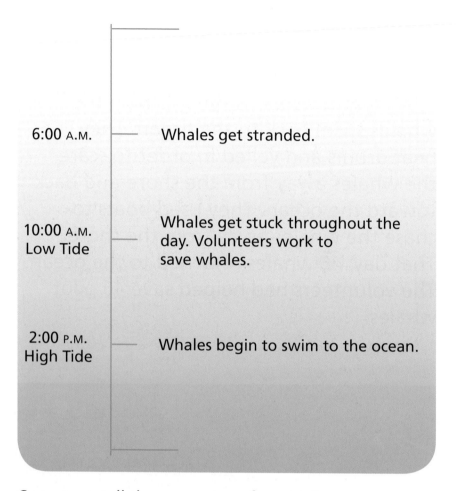

|  |  |
|---|---|
| 6:00 A.M. | Whales get stranded. |
| 10:00 A.M. Low Tide | Whales get stuck throughout the day. Volunteers work to save whales. |
| 2:00 P.M. High Tide | Whales begin to swim to the ocean. |

Can you retell the sequence of events?

Scientists believe that whales sometimes swim toward shore because they are looking for food. Whales like to eat fish that live near the coast.

More whales probably will be stranded in the future. But we can hope that many people will come to help them.